Instant Scrum

Instant Scrum

Andrew White

Preface

This book has been written with the sole intent of
allowing you speed of access to the information
which you require.
The author has achieved this by writing in a grid
pattern style.

All things in life can be represented in a grid.

Thank you.

Table of Contents

Contents

Example Sprint with events

code	Event/act
S	daily scrum event
Rev	Sprint review event
Ret	Sprint retro event
Plan	Sprint planning event
SB	Sprint backlog act

	8am	9	10	11	12	13	14	15	16:00
Mon			S				SB		
Tues			Rev	Rev	Rev		Ret	Ret	Ret
Wed			S	Plan	Plan		Plan	Plan	Plan
Thur			S						
Friday			S						
Sat									
Sun									
Mon			S						
Tues			S						
Wed			S						
Thur			S						
Friday			S						
Sat									
Sun									
Mon			S				SB		
Tues			Rev	Rev	Rev		Ret	Ret	Ret
Wed			S	Plan	Plan		Plan	Plan	Plan

Sprint

Description	Container for all the events
Sequence	1st
Duration	Up to 1 month (usually 2 weeks)
Inputs	Definition of what is to be built A design A flexible plan
Processing	No changes are made that would endanger the Sprint goal Quality goals do not decrease Scope may be clarified & re-negotiated between PO & Dev as more is learned
Outputs	Sprint backlog Working increment
Notes	Product owner can cancel the Sprint (if Sprint goal becomes obsolete)
	Dev Team deliver an increment of productivity at every Sprint
	All Scrum Teams working on same product do not have to have the same Sprint length
	Sprint starts immediately after conclusion of the previous Sprint
	Sprint length decided by Scrum Team at Sprint Retro

Sprint Planning

	Inspection and adapt event
Description	the work to be performed in the Sprint is planned at the Sprint Planning
Sequence	2nd
Duration	8 hours or less
Frequency	Meet once per Sprint cycle (after retro)
Attendees mandatory	Scrum Team
Attendees optional	Key stakeholders Technical or domain advice from invited people
Inputs	Latest product increment Projected capacity of the Dev Team during the Sprint Past performance of the Dev Team
Processing	Dev decomposes work Product owner agrees scope of next Sprint (What) can be delivered in the upcoming Sprint (how) will the work needed to deliver the increment be achieved
Outputs	Forecast of functionality Sprint goal Sprint backlog
Notes	Dev explains to P.O. & S.M. how they intend to accomplish the Sprint goal and create anticipated increment
	Prod backlog items that can be 'done' by Dev Team within one Sprint are deemed 'ready' for selection in a Sprint planning session

Daily Scrum

	Inspection and adapt event
Description	A 15-minute time-boxed event for the Development Team to synchronize activities and create a plan for the next 24 hours
Sequence	3rd
Duration	up to 15 minutes
Frequency	daily
Attendees mandatory	Dev Team
Attendees optional	Prod owner (as a spectator) Scrum master (as a spectator)
Inputs	Inspect the work since the last daily scrum
Processing	Usually; What I did yesterday to reach Sprint goal What I will do today to reach Sprint goal Any impediment from reaching Sprint goal
Outputs	Optimise probability that Dev Team will meet Sprint goal Create a Sprint plan for the next 24 hours Progress shown in Sprint Backlog Forecasting the work that could be done before the next Daily Scrum Improved communication Eliminates other meetings Identify impediments to Dev for removal Highlights/promotes quick decision making
Notes	There is no prescribed structure
	Cannot be skipped

Sprint Review

description	Informal inspect & adapt event – not a status meeting inspect the Increment and adapt the Product Backlog
Sequence	4th (before retro)
Duration	=<4 hours
frequency	Meet once per Sprint cycle
Attendees mandatory	Scrum Master Dev Product Owner (no representatives are allowed)
Attendees optional	Invited key stakeholders (they are invited by Product Owner)
Inputs	Product increment (to elicit feedback)
Processing	Collaborate on next thing that optimises value Product owner forecasts product burndown Adapt the product backlog if needed Dev Team demos what has been done & answers questions about the increment Product owner explains what prod backlog items have & have not been done Product owner discusses the prod backlog
Outputs	Next things that optimise value Revised prod backlog items that define the probable prod backlog for the next Sprint Progress of product increment ascertained Timeline budget Potential capabilities Marketplace for next anticipated release

Sprint Retro

	Inspection and adapt event
Description	an opportunity for the Scrum Team to inspect itself and create a plan for improvements to be enacted during the next Sprint
Sequence	5th (after review but before planning)
Duration	=<3 hours for 1month Sprints
Frequency	Meet once per Sprint cycle
Attendees mandatory	Scrum Master (as peer Team member) Product Owner Dev Team
Attendees optional	Invited key stakeholders (they are invited by Product Owner)
Inputs	Last Sprint
Processing	Scrum Team to inspect itself and plan Facilitate inspection and adaption Adapt (change) Definition of Done Inspect how last Sprint went with people, relationships, processes and tools Identify & order the major items that went well & potential improvements
Outputs	A changed 'Definition of Done' by Scrum Team A plan for implementing improvements to the way the scrum Team does its work Sprint length
Notes	Process and people orientated

Scrum Master

Description	Manages scrum framework
Part of	Scrum Team Could be part of Dev Team

Owner of	Promoting and supporting Scrum
	Servant-hearted leadership
	Educator of product owner
	Enforcing rule that only Dev Team
	  members participate in Daily Scrum
	Scrum framework
	Ensuring daily scrum takes place & is
	  timeboxed to 15 minutes
	Facilitating discussions within the Dev
	  Team
	Coping with incomplete artefact
	  transparency

Roles	Plans scrum implementation within
	  an organisation
	Working with other Scrum Masters to
	  increase effectiveness within an
	  organisation
	Leading & coaching the organisation in its
	  Scrum adoption

Notes	Participates in Sprint Retro as peer Team member

Product Owner

description	is responsible for maximizing the value of the product resulting from the work of the Development Team
Part of	Scrum Team Could be part of Dev

Owner of	The sole authority to cancel a Sprint (invariably
	    because Sprint goal becomes obsolete)
	Solely responsible for managing the
	    product backlog

Roles	Provides transparency via product
	    backlog
	Makes changes to product backlog
	At Sprint review – explains what prod
	    backlog items have/have not been done
	Monitoring the remaining work towards
	    the project goal
	During Sprint planning negotiates scope
	    of what the Team will work on next

Events	Sprint planning Sprint review
Acts	Product backlog refinement
Notes	Product value maximiser
	One PO per product/project

Dev Team

Description	consists of professionals who do the work of delivering a potentially releasable Increment of "Done" product at the end of each Sprint
Part of	Scrum Team
Owner of	Conducting the Daily Scrum Estimation of product backlog items Definition of Done Tracking work remaining in Sprint Sprint review - demos what/what not done Answering questions about the increment Modifying Sprint backlog Inspections of work Forecasting the functionality that will be developed during the Sprint Organising and managing their own work
Roles	Convert product backlog into a working product increment
Events	Daily Scrum Sprint planning
Acts	Product backlog refinement
Inputs	Selects product backlog items for the Sprint
Processing	Can modify prod backlog under permission of the Product Owner
Outputs	Potentially shippable increment every Sprint Accomplish the Sprint goal Definition of Done (during Sprint Retro)
Notes	3 to 9 members
	Cross-functional – all the skills to ship
	No sub Teams
	Accountability belongs to Team as a whole
	No Job titles other than 'Dev'

Scrum Team

Description	Consists of;
	  Dev Team,
	  Product Owner,
	  Scrum Master

Owner of	making definition of done changing definition of done in Sprint retro crafting the Sprint goal at Sprint planning
Notes	All Scrum Teams working on the same product do not have to have aligned Sprints

	Team model is designed to have;
	  Flexibility,
	  Creativity,
	  Productivity

Sprint backlog

Description	A scrum artefact A set of prod backlog items that were selected for the Sprint during Sprint Planning (plus the plan for delivering them) A plan for delivering the product increment & realising the Sprint goal A forecast by the Dev Team about what functionality will be in the next increment & the work needed to deliver that functionality into a 'Done' increment
Owned by	Dev Team
Belongs to	Dev Team
Inputs	Product backlog items
Processing	Dev Team modifies Sprint backlog throughout the Sprint Dev Team adds new work to the Sprint backlog Only Dev can change its Sprint backlog during a sprint
Outputs	Backlog items, related tasks, estimations
Notes	If new work is added during a Sprint then estimated remaining work will increase
	All dev Teams working on same product will each have their own separate Sprint backlogs
	Dev Team can create new work & add it
	Dev Team can represent Sprint backlog in any way that it chooses

Refinement - Product backlog refinement

Description	Source of requirements for any changes to be made to the product
Attendees	Product owner Dev Team
Owned by	Product owner
Belongs to	Product owner
Events	This not a scrum event
Acts	Product backlog refinement is a scrum act
Inputs	Product backlog
Processing	Items are reviewed & revised Scrum Team decides how & when Product backlog refinement is done Dev Team responsible for all estimates (Prod Owner can influence this)
Output	Usually consumes up to 10% of capacity of Dev Team Refined product backlog items – attributes; Description, order, estimate, value Usually less valuable/most unclear at bottom
Notes	Prod Backlog is never complete
	Prod backlog can be updated at any time by Prod owner
	Evolves with product – needs to be appropriate
	Exists as long as the product exists
	Is dynamic
	An inspection & adaption act
	All Dev Teams working on the same product should use the same product backlog

Definition of Done

Description	A standard used by Scrum Team to assess if a product increment is 'Done'
Created by	Scrum Team
Events	Sprint retro is where DoD is changed by the Scrum Team
Processing	DoD can be changed in Sprint Retro by Scrum Team
Output	Access when work is complete on the product increment Helps to identify unfinished work in a Sprint
Notes	DoD should not contain conditions that are not completely within the influence of the Scrum Team
	DoD provides a checklist to take the increment close to production deployable state
	As Scrum Teams mature DoD will expand to include more stringent criteria for higher Quality
	Ensures artefact transparency
	Anything required for the product increment to be production fit must be part of the DoD
Example;	Developer Tested
	Unit Tests created/maintained and pass
	Local integration tests pass
	Build details completed on Jira card
	Release spreadsheet updated
	Code review performed
	Deployed to correct QA environment
	Acceptance tests pass
	Product owner has reviewed and signed off
	Release card created (where applicable)

Stakeholder

Description	A person external to the Scrum Team with a specific interest in & knowledge of a product that is required for incremental discovery
Notes	Not part of the Scrum Team
	Can be invited to the Sprint Retro
	Can be invited to Sprint Review

Scrum Theory

Foundation	Empirical process control theory
Description	A small Team of people that is highly flexible and adaptive There are three pillars of empiricism; transparency, inspection, adaption
Transparency	Common language common definition of 'done' for those accepting the work product
Inspection	Frequently inspect Scrum artefacts and progress towards a Sprint goal
Adaption	Inspector decides if aspects or process is outside acceptable limits – making the product unacceptable If so, then an adjustment must be made ASAP
Events	There are four inspection and adaption events; Sprint Planning, Daily Scrum, Sprint Review, Sprint Retro
Notes	Allows additional meetings if they facilitate the Sprint goal
	The three qualities that the Team model in Scrum is designed to optimise are; Productivity, creativity, flexibility
	Scrum comprises of; rules, events, roles, artefacts

Sprint cancellation

Description	Cancellation of the Sprint
Owned by	Product owner
Inputs	Sprint
Processing	Cancelled by Product Owner only if the sprint goal becomes obsolete
Output	After Sprint cancellation; Any completed & 'done' prod backlog items are reviewed. If part of the work is potentially releasable the Product owner typically accepts it. All complete product backlog items are re-estimated & put back on the prod backlog

Values

Description	Commitment Courage Focus Openness Respect

Sprint Goal

Description	Provides guidance to the Team on why it is building the increment
Created by	Scrum Team during 'what' section of Sprint Planning
Notes	In Scrum additional meetings are allowed if they facilitate the Sprint goal
	The expression of Sprint goal is a business need (business speak)

Qualities

Description	Creativity Productivity Flexibility

Pillars of empiricism

description	Decisions are based upon observation, experience and experimentation
pillars	Transparency Inspection Adaption

Artefact transparency

Description	the degree of openness (apparent ability to inspect & adapt); the Sprint Increment the Sprint Backlog the Product Backlog
Owner	Scrum Master
Notes	Scrum Master is responsible for coping with incomplete artefact transparency

Increment

Description	Sum of all the prod backlog items completed during the Sprint & the value of the increments of all previous sprints
Created by	Dev Team
Outputs	Each increment contains only 'Done' functionality that could be released (not necessarily to live) immediately

Inspection and adapt

Description	Key inspect and adapt events are; Sprint planning Daily scrum Sprint review Sprint retro

Participation

Description	People outside the scrum Team are allowed to participate in; Sprint planning (key stakeholders, technical or domain advice from invited people) Sprint review (invited (by P.O.) key stakeholders)

Estimation method

Description	Scrum does not prescribe any specific estimation method

Scrum events

Description	Sprint (container for the other events) up to 1 month Sprint planning; <=8 hours Daily scrum; 15 minutes Sprint review; <=4 hours Sprint retro; <=3 hours

Scrum artefacts

Description	Product backlog Sprint backlog increment
Notes	Scrum Master coaches the Team to increase the transparency of the artefacts

Scrum Acts

Description	Product backlog refinement

Team velocity

Description	Average of amount of product backlog items turned into 'Done' items per Sprint

Forecast of functionality

Description	The selection of items from the product backlog that a dev Team deems feasible for implementation in a Sprint
Owner	Dev Team

Burn up / Burn down

Description	Burn up shows increase in completion Burn down shows remaining effort

Notes

Notes

Notes

Notes

Notes

www.ingramcontent.com/pod-product-compliance
Lightning Source LLC
Chambersburg PA
CBHW031232050326
40689CB00009B/1578

* 9 7 8 1 0 9 0 7 0 4 3 7 5 *